SPRINKLES FROM THE HEART

A HARMONIUS JOURNEY THROUGH LIFE, LOVE AND NATURE'S SEASONS

A POETRY ODYSSEY

SHIVA MALEKOPMATH

BlueRose ONE.com
Stories Matter
NewDelhi • London

BLUEROSE PUBLISHERS
India | U.K.

BlueRose ONE
Stories Matter
NewDelhi • London

For permissions requests or inquiries regarding this publication, please contact:

BLUEROSE PUBLISHERS
www.BlueRoseONE.com
info@bluerosepublishers.com
+91 8882 898 898
+4407342408967

ISBN: 978-93-6261-091-1

Cover Design: Basavraj Neljeri
Typesetting: Pooja Sharma

First Edition: May 2024

DEDICATION

TO MY PARENTS

SHRI V. R. MALEKOPMATH

SMT KUSUM V MALEKOPMATH

&

TO MY IN- LAWS

SHRI CHANNAMALLAYA HIREMATH (RAPATI)

SMT SULOCHANA C HIREMATH (RAPATI)

Foreword

Man springs from nature but lives apart,
Tries to fathom both mind and heart,
Expresses thoughts, oft in prose,
But in their hearts everyone knows
That poetry strikes the right note.
In any case it gets my vote.
Shiva Malekopmath ranges far and wide.
Varied thoughts he takes in his stride.
Desire, love, spiritual longing
Both estrangement and belonging.
Broken hearts he'd like to heal.
But at the end of the day, I feel
What he really want to see
Is being merged with eternity.
If spirituality is sought,
Read his book, learn his thought.
As you wander, you will wonder!

I'll say no more, nor steal his thunder!

Plunge right in, spend some time,

Learn from his rhythm and his rhyme!

Nadir Godrej

Industrialist & Chairman

Godrej Group

Introduction of Ashok Hiremath

In the luminous tapestry of life, where diverse threads weave the story of existence, Shiva Malekopmath emerges as a soulful craftsman, seamlessly blending the worlds of philosophy, social work, and poetry. "Sprinkles from the Heart," a collection of poems penned by Shiva, invites readers to embark on a poignant journey through the corridors of his contemplative mind.

Beyond the conventional labels that society may attach, Shiva Malekopmath is a modern-day polymath. His endeavors span the realms of industry, social work, yoga instruction, and the heartfelt expression found in his blog, "Shiva's Ponder," where his verses find resonance with a wide audience eager to explore the depths of the human experience.

This collection is an exploration of the delicate nuances of life, love, and introspection, where Shiva's verses serve as gentle whispers from the heart. While his engagements as a social worker and yoga teacher shape the world around him, his poetry delves into the realms of emotion, spirituality, and the interconnectedness of all things.

"Sprinkles from the Heart" is not merely a book of poems; it is an offering of insights into the essence of being. Shiva's words, like gentle sprinkles, land softly on the reader's soul, provoking thought and stirring the

emotions. Each poem is a brushstroke on the canvas of shared human experience, capturing the universal truths that connect us all.

As you turn the pages of this collection, be prepared to be transported into a world where Shiva's reflections become mirrors for your own contemplation. "Sprinkles from the Heart" is an invitation to savor the beauty of simplicity, explore the depths of introspection, and immerse yourself in the timeless wisdom that flows from the heart of a philosopher-poet whose words resonate with the shared heartbeat of humanity.

Ashok Hiremath

Industrialist &

Founder Astec Sciences Ltd

Preface

It is such a Great moment for me that the thoughts have now transformed into this Book which I have titled as "Sprinkles From The Heart". My Blog "theshivasponder.wordpress.com" has given me all the encouragement and boost to pen my thoughts more and more as I published time and again. Thanks once again to all my ardent readers.

I started writing late in life, maybe an occasion was required to pen down the thoughts. My immediate family, Wife and Daughters gave me all the support and care while I was not in good health. I take this as an opportunity to thank those Dear ones.

Writing does require Good Reading, it is a basic qualification. Even in my busy schedule of running a business I took time to read and then write. Origin of thoughts from the Author is the most essential pre-requisite condition.

I would like to thank some of the most important beings here for the help and support they gave me. Deb Cowdrey a very committed blogger at WordPress gave me all the support while I was blogging, she encouraged me through her comments always. Hema Subramanian a very old friend of mine through the Rotaract Club of which I was the DRR during the year 1978 - 79. Shri Prasad Patil of Hubli who came like God sent man and helped me to send manuscript and other computer related things. My special thanks to Artist Basavraj Neljeri of Gadag who crafted the cover page.

I Sincerely thank Shri Nadir Godrej the Chairman of the Godrej Conglomerate and Shri Ashok Hiremath founder of the Astec Sciences Company both are very busy persons who after reading my Poems have given The Best Foreword and Introduction. You can observe in the Foreword of Mr Godrej that he has written in Poetry style. He himself writes poetry and shares it among his friends. Let us hope he brings out his own Book of Poems.

I also thank Blue Rose for their commitment to encourage people like me to publish their own works. On a personal note I wish them All the Very Best.

Thanks for having this Book in your hands, take time to read and ponder the thoughts. Let's be calm and cool, living the moment brings mindfulness. Applying Our Intelligence to every moment is being Human and Worth it.

Let Sprinkled drops of thoughts bring Solace.

Shiva Malekopmath
shivamalekopmath@gmail.com

Sprinkled Droplets for You

01 Love and To Be Loved

Oh! My Angel..Manifest!

I cried it seems
As I came in this world
Eyes not yet opened
Who was there in the midst?
For sure my Mother
The Nurses and Doctor
Then came everyone
Have been in their presence since
Every step I moved
I did not know
That there was someone
Who Watched & Protected me
I have done things Good, Bad and Worst
I Walked, Ran and Stumbled
Someone stopped me
Doing further Bad and Worst things
That invisible Hand and Eyes showed
The Path to follow
Experience and Knowledge
Tells me to Ponder
Who is with You
All this while
Till this moment
That there is an Angel
Imperceptible and Inconspicuous
Unnoticeably in Disguise

Now I am sure
You are there
You are here and everywhere isn't?
With you I have fallen in Love
Before I close my eyes
Oh! My Angel Manifest

❖

Those Moments are Enough

Those moments are Enough
For the rest of my Life

Holding you Abreast
In my arms for you to Rest
These days are the Best

I have become insensible of Time
What can I do if others think its a Crime
For they know not; its for me so Prime

I take in your breathed Air
Inhaling it, intoxicates but its Fair
Are we not committed to Bear

Light emitting from thine Eyes
Messages received from the Skies
Buried in the Hearts it Lies

I am lost, in this Bliss
To come out from, I shall Miss
Let anyone call me, I shall Hiss

We are tied in the Love Belt
I am cool, in your warmth I melt.
Did you feel about it and Smelt?

Forgetting all Nuances
Those days have now been Reminiscences
The collective Remembrances

In future shall be Commemorations

Those moments are Enough
For the rest of my Life

❖

Distant Heart

A call from the Distant Heart
From a World Apart

Bodies that never Met
Wished wings they couldn't Get

Minds craving to meet and Flourish
Circumstances could not Accomplish

Tears flow on each other's Face
But with a smile in the Grace

No regrets for being Divided
Its Time that Decided

Time not in existence for Both
Into togetherness they took the Oath

Thinking of each other in Eternity
Love for one another in Entirety

Soulmates meet on Earth
In Heaven, if not, it is its Dearth

No Body required, they Meet Anywhere
No Place required, they Meet Everywhere

❖

Healer of the Broken Hearts

I see
I go astray
For I see broken hearts
Everywhere and wherever
For once they were full of Love
Shaped diamond shinning
Into pieces
Lost its grandeur
Quality not deteriorated
For still the Love persists
Hearts left alone
But full of Love
No doubt
Craving to be again
In the love
Want of response
Self pride pushing back
Wishes & Ambitions sword played
Thus broke Hearts in pieces
I stand no more
To see
Them parted
What meaning love
Shall carry
Continuance of situation
Shall inspire no one

To love in future
Hence I beg
Give me the Cross, Jesus!
Oh! Shiva! your Trishul
Or something divine
Even a stick
The Power
Shall work
For I want to be
Healer of the Broken Hearts

❖

Two Beloveds

Love

Two Awesome

I Love You

Eye Contact Brought Closer

Murmuring In Each Others Arms

Affection Was So Strong And Thick

Smelling, Cuddling, Touching, Feeling Came The Way

Olfactory, Visual, Auditory, Gustatory, Kinesthetic Senses Derived Pleasure

Time Passed By, Quarrels, Hatred, Misunderstandings, Uncompassionate Made Apart

Two Souls Realised Waiting To Reunite Until Death Bell Rang

Have Met Each Other For A Long Lasting Relationship Forever

The Waiting For Lives Gone Until Unification That Formed

Understanding Was Clear Both Of Them Could Hear

Happiness, Bliss Came All The Way Through

Senses Have No Part To Play

Prayer, Meditation, Chanting In Process

Not Seen Each Other

That Made Them

No Two

Love

Why You

Of the Billions that are there
Of the Millions that I come across
Of the Thousands that I meet and talk
Why You
I Love You
My Beloved
Of the Trillions that You created
Of the Millions of species You formed
Of the Thousands who pray for You
Why You
Love Me too
My Beloved

'..The 'Coming' Ends

You want Me to come to You
You know it is such a hardship
You come to Me
I shall snuggle into You, forever
Then shall there be no 'coming', it ends.

❖

Your Arms Like Octopussy Tentacles

Your arms like octopussy tentacles
griped me into your fold.

Unaware of facts of love
stunned to see myself in goosebumps.

Intimacy to the core of fondness
magic of fascination turns into inflorescence.

Eyes locked to unlock chapters
of the love saga in the making.

Deep in the blanket of love
silent inner spirits feel the warmth.

Sudden shift in nature's attitude turns conducive
music of nature brings pleasure adds essence to the rendezvous.

Two bodies welded to become one
from time zone have gone into timeless.

All senses extract joy and pleasure
bodies yearned and are enthralled.

Devoid of desire to be in earthly realms
eternity be in your arms like octopussy tentacles.

❖

Accelerated Heart Beats

Accelerated heart beats remember the first embrace

Produced such joy and bliss, love and affection

Memory still fresh as newly grown grass and dew drops

Aura of the essence, body odor, perception, compatibility

Forever let it be so, intensity of the thought, feeling and apprehension

Accelerated heart beats remember of death so near

Produced fastness in breath and blood circulation, thought process and ardor

Memory of past, ebb & flow, peaks & valleys of life, systole and diastole of heart

Aura of divinity within, sanctity of life, righteousness
Forever to dissolve in eternity, a benediction

❖

02 For One to Ponder

Celestial Embrace

My arms wide open
My thoughts, and
My covetous eyes
To Embrace
The Vast, Blissful, Universe
The Irresistible long wait
The Coming and Going
In My Apprehension, to
Forget and Dissolve, to
Unveil the screen Amid
Being in the midst for Millenniums
Was in Aplomb, to
Be one with You, now
You have come as My Consort
As if the outcome of my Penance
Quintessentially in form
Is that in Disguise?
In Flesh and Blood, with
The Warmth of your Body and Heart
The Petrichor emitting from your body
I Snuggled into You
Our bodies Entwined
The Texture of your skin

The Nectar from your lips and tongue
The Essence of the Divine
Compassion on this Terra
Your Voice, Speech and Language
A Celestial Music
Your presence a Fervour, Aroma, Incense
Your Human embrace
Makes me feel
Am no more being Human
In your Being, Infinity and Bliss
I would want to Disembody
I feel Embodied, in
Your Celestial Embrace

❖

I Cease to See

The Beautiful People in the world
The Love in all Hearts
The Innocence in the Kids
The Appearance of Colours
In Flowers and Paints
In Trees and Nature
The Sunrise and Sunsets
The explicit Words
The touch of Warmth
The breath of Life
The Taste of lovingly cooked Food
The Landscapes, Art and Art forms
The Animals and Birds
The Aqua and Marine life
The Frantic Past
The Bombastic Future
Trivial to the Present
Experience, Enjoy and Feel the Now
The Aversion to Hate and Negativity
Waste not a second
Seconds pass by
In their own Pace
Counted are those

Gratitude to My Mother & Mother Earth

Grateful to All who have come my way

Thanks Millions, to

My Body, My Family, My In-Laws

The Journey to unknown Realms

Nearby it comes Exponential

When God of Death

Shall take me Away

I Cease to See

❖

Once Upon a Time

<u>Once Upon A Time —- Just Born</u>
Pound of flesh full life
Fresh as morning full promises
Wrinkled skin closed eyes
Sound of cry to live life ahead
<u>Once Upon A Time — 6 Months</u>
Bright eyes penetrates heart
Smell of flesh fragrant deep breaths
Carried by all kisses received everywhere
Mother's warmth fed for life
<u>Once Upon A Time — One Year</u>
Standing on legs balancing life
Innocence spills showered by love
Being lovely dressed wetting clothes
First year birth celebration passes by
<u>Once Upon A Time —3 Years</u>
Holding hands walking straight
Taught by signs learning language
Done wrong or right hugged and kissed
World wonders seen wonders world see
<u>Once Upon A Time — 5 Years</u>
Ready to school thoughts of play
First friends meet no blood relationships start
Teacher's word ultimate life homeworks begin

Joy at peak world influence untouched

<u>Once Upon A Time — 9 Years</u>

Mischievous traits talent artistic aptitude show up

Right and wrong societal venom infuse

Getting smarter to be among smart world

Enthusiasm brings joy playful learning process

<u>Once Upon A Time — 14 Years</u>

Body metabolism changes felt

Sense of attraction towards other sex

Focus on deeds getting sharper

Ambitions start building up

<u>Once Upon A Time — 18 Years</u>

Emotions sentiments start making marks

Relationships formed remain in mind evermore

Grandiosity of appearance opulence of good health evince

All the more urge to love and to be loved

<u>Once Upon A Time — 21 Years</u>

Fixing goals actions to accomplish

Economic gains foremost priority

New circle of friends gala time

Good and bad habits form seeking pleasure

<u>Once Upon A Time — 30 Years</u>

Choosing life partner offsprings result

Life immersed in toto into worldly affairs

Best of times being spent

Success achieved aspiration to attain more successes

<u>Once Upon A Time — 45 Years</u>

Stress strain erupt from working and home ends

Life responsibilities at its peak

Materialistic accumulations all for happy moments
Sincere efforts hard work law of nature presents fruits

<u>Once Upon A Time — 60 Years</u>

Looking back life passed like a jiffy
Not all fortunately some tend towards spirituality
Memories bring solace agony of past times
Time in abundance for relaxation

<u>Once Upon A Time — 75 Years</u>

Most friends relatives vanish from scene
Wrinkled skin looks change unimaginable
Disease and disorders uninvited guests
Enhanced zeal to live cheerfully in smiles

<u>Once Upon A Time — 90 Years</u>

Back into cradle again but a little big
Feeble body fragile mind is the plight
Dependence to lead and conduct life
Consciousness still inspiring and illustrious

<u>Once Upon A Time — After Death</u>

Remembrances commemorations celebrate some for few days
Kith and kin crave in hearts times well spent
At places loved ones hang photos on wall seen in albums too
Once upon a time it all happens in human life

❖

One Dust Particle!

Millions, Trillions
Cosmos fits in
Planets, Stars, Moons, Suns
Living, Dead
Imagination spells enormous
Size Capacity Vastness
Spell bound when known
Earth
One Dust Particle! One Dust Particle!! One Dust Particle!!!

Close Earth Looks
Human Behaviour
Engrossed & Involved
Pride Ego Play
Act Big, Feel Big
In Time & Space
Being on Earth
Infinity Says
Earth
One Dust Particle! One Dust Particle!! One Dust Particle!!!

Human Act
Against Nature
Birds Trees Animals Life

Millenniums Past

In tune with Nature

All living backed by

One Source, One Energy

In the Cosmos

Oh! Human Remember!!!

Earth

One Dust Particle! One Dust Particle!! One Dust Particle!!!

Millions, Trillions

Cells in Body

Reverse Thought

Close Observation & Study

Science shows

Minutest Particles

Deeper exploration

Found Atom, Protons, Neutrons

Spell again Infinity

Me being One, on

Earth

One Dust Particle! One Dust Particle!! One Dust Particle!!!

I & Life Fight; Peacefully

I Fight
With Life
It Fights with Me
We have Fought enough
There were better tournaments
To Participate, Play and Win
I have won few
It has won few
Sometimes there was a draw
Its not like we do not fight anymore
Maybe both are fed up with each other
Both ask each other - why fight?
And we both agreed
Life goes on
So, Life and I go peacefully

Concrete Jungle Night

Concrete jungle night seen far, dead silent atmosphere

Sparkling, glowing, gleaming, dim, dark lights

Presence of life spell, moving automotives red bright lights

What not during night, drink and dance parties, murders, debauchery, deals, crimes all evil sorts

Night being such wonderful time, undisturbed sleep, meditation, virtuous acts so on

Unlike humans, animals, birds in peaceful hours get energised for tomorrow

Some for some best dreams may come true and is good during late hours

Shame on humans, make night conducive for improper, illegal activities

Human engaged always takes lot from nature gives back crap

❖

One Day is Over

ONE DAY IS OVER
YOU SAY & YOU THINK
YOU HAVE YOUR NIGHTS
YOU PARTY AND DANCE
YOU HAVE YOUR SUPPER AND GO TO SLEEP
YOU SEE & YOU IMAGINE

I AM HIDDEN IN THE CLOUDS
I AM MORNING AGAIN
I AM IN THE OTHER PART OF THE WORLD
I SHINE THERE FOR THEM TO LIVE
I DID FOR YOU TODAY
I THINK HAVE YOU EVER THOUGHT FOR MY REST
I AM THE SUN

❖

..In this Stupid Body

In the womb, with the smallest legs in this world
Kicking right & left
Giving all the pain & pleasure too
Growing there as fast & wanting to come out
Crying came out & showering happiness all over
Received kisses from elderly girls, women & men too
All carried here & there like a ball in their hands
As if the ball being a symbol of love & cuddling
Hugs & hugging went on for long
Play & games was in the routine
Then came schooling & the mates
Went on getting education & knowledge too
Earning for a living & have a family too
Apart from the legs, hands & body there is a mind too
This mind dreaming of necessary & unnecessary things too
Some have come true & some have not
Deriving pleasure & happiness for the senses
Being the order of the day, this & everything else
Days & years passing by, realising now as to what to do
Forgetting the past & remembering a little too
The body having trillions of cells & ofcourse living in that too
Millions daily taking birth & billions dying too
So makes this body old & not as before

Seeing other older bodies helpless & hopeless

Question arises... & this body also going to be one so

The thought makes one frighten & shivering too

The body would not permit & allow too

Blinking the eyes to open & to see life has gone by

To wish & work like before

To accomplish & to attain as dreamt

Life goes on & on

Who is this? Thoughts pouring now & then

Thinking got the answer..... its I .... in this stupid body.

❖

My Ungrateful Life

Millions at work for me for my life
Humans, animals, birds, bees, eggs,fish, insects, trees and plants
Farm produce, animal food, milk, oil, honey, aqua food and fruits
All for my best of living and comforts
One more day sanctioned to breathe prana the life-giving force
I consume with no gratitude
I am ashamed for mine is an ungrateful life

❖

..The Sky Wonders at Me

I see, the Sky Wonders at Me
It watches me
By birth
I landed beneath it
From then on
The here and there
The wandering with or without purpose
It also knows I am not a vagabond
Witnessing day and night
The love I share
The instant anger and temperament
It knows everything
I am in good health, happy and overwhelmed
I am sick and sad
I am scared, sorrowful and disgusted
I am puzzled
I am confused
I work hard, at times lazy
I am with all
I am alone
There is no secret I can hide
It has no place for it to hide
My head tilts up

I stretch my arms wide towards
It stretches so wide as if
To swallow me and the world
I ask who are You
Who am I?
It is silent
Silently it says
I am transcendence
I am the bliss
I am there forever
You come and go
It says as if
It has said so many times
Can you not hear me?
I am left still thinking
Meanwhile
The Sky Wonders at Me

❖

Sands of Time

Time immemorial, time to time existence in form passed away.

Humans for a while are a memory in hearts of loved

In whom they are memory they also passed in the sands of time

In times's grip are all, nothing without the clutch

Time sweeps all beings alongwith, try to know, it has gone by

Not a single left behind to see, only dust or in wide sky or in the heavens

While in present everything looks beautiful, wonderful, enchanting, admirable, and lovely

Everything becomes earth, dust, soil, air

Acceptance of time of what it shows now, or else, no wait, it flies makes a tale

❖

Death-Next Moment

Death is invariably the next moment
No one perceives when it's arrival time
Inevitable when comes its next moment
Animals can't contemplate death
Exalted man contemplates death at ease
Conquers inner world attains ever bliss
For him there is no fear of death

Storm of Troubles

Like storm they come creating blackout

Shaking my thoughts inserting awful feelings

Pulling my basement make me shudder to breathe for life

I stand by my robust stem and roots

They shy in shame go out of sight for a while

In habit of creating hell on earth

Hiding and seeking craving to step-in

Only to come to see my daring tough looks

I possess no rooms for unwanted guests

Solution lasts for them is only to escape

Exploring

Blinking lights stop
Wifi router says
You are lost
My right elbow rests
On the computer table
Left palm on forehead
Blinking my eyes on
Tells me you are lost in eternity
Continue questioning
Will there be a comeback?
OMG!
Inquisitiveness plays role
Mind wanting to reach out
Helpless in silence
Voice from inside echoes
If there was a mantra
To make it a comeback
No in vain says another
By then, the lights blink
My eyes stop the blink
Happy as ever
Throwing myself like the net
How a fisherman throws his net

Into the waters

Of the world again

Exploring

❖

So..That's Enough

A thousand bullets in the Heart
Attempt to Count
Shall add thousands more
Bodily injuries healed and gone, since
Reminiscences tell, injuries at Heart
Deep and Red hot
Covered by Ashes
Bullets sprayed by the Loved ones, and
In Society they are as much
Have torn my Heart Apart
They still shall Spray, yet
I live by the courage Installed
Shall HE extend the Age?
Bless in Perfect health
Another 100 years or two
HE shall not, I am sure
Every morning I pray, take ME away
So..that's Enough.

The Hourglass

Other day I purchased one hourglass a scarce commodity now

Looks simple antique vintage designed calls on for attraction

Made of brass superannuated letters engraved also says London 1885

Glass blocks sand known for transparency

It has been my latest play; sand falls down inverted starts again

Sand particles minute, every drop depicts gravity, heaps of sand change shape

Fascination for device watcher's time stands still in enchantment

Flow smooth though, time runs out particles reveal fraction of seconds

With it during play stunned to know life moves so fast

Ordinarily in life's tenure its obscure, OMG! Time flies such speed

Amazing! Sand being pulled down concludes one time measure! Humans being pulled by sensual pleasures complete one cycle of life

Many such products or things inspire us to correct life in realization of blissful state

Ancient timing tool likewise has many things to tell and teach – THE HOURGLASS

Death-Next Moment

Death is invariably the next moment
No one perceives when it's arrival time
Inevitable when comes its next moment
Animals can't contemplate death
Exalted man contemplates death at ease
Conquers inner world attains ever bliss
For him there is no fear of death

Sorrow – Most Private Affair

I am not complaining either
As you are not also
One that Liveth
He/She that Loveth
Has had his share of sorrow
The one that one shall not share
As deep in Heart its hidden
One would heck to know
Would want to measure
Could anyone find the device?
Of the sea of tears, pain and displeasure
You imagined it
You created it
You formed it
For the sake of Love
For the Heck of it
But dear Sorrow
Has been part of Life
Yes its been So
Who is going to Stop anyway
I know you Suffer
I know you are also Sorrowful
To share

You would not want
I would also not
We have kept the world out of it to reach
As everyone has this affair in Private
All only for themselves
Would not want to show the world
Living life's journey
In their own Music
Let it go back in the muds
No bother it shall remain
In the sands of Time
Yes it is Your Private affair
Yes it is My Private affair

❖

What's More

What more expect from nature
Wonders of World enough
Human is one such Wonder

Where Shall I Be Taken? The Quest Remains

My Quest to know
Never evaporates
Mingled in the body
Tingled by the Karma
Condoned ill health
Pardoned the sinful
Forgave the graceless
Overlooked the rude
Crossing the river of Life
Where shall I be taken?
The Quest Remains

Black Holes, Galaxies, Innumerable Universes
Thus in the vast abode
I shall dwell in peace
I do not care where
The Murderers, Dishonest, Wicked, Deceit have been taken
But am worried where
The People with Love, Truth, and Honesty sent
Countless have gone from here
Even Saints, Sufis, Sants, Rishis and Martyrs
Where shall I be taken?
The Quest Remains

Eyes wide open nights

In full consciousness

Like an insomniac

Buried in the thoughts

Of after leaving this body

Make me listen a lullaby

Make me know

So I shall sleep well

Have sweet dreams of the thought

Where shall I be taken?

The Quest Remains

03 The Spiritual Being

Celestial Embrace

My arms wide open
My thoughts, and
My covetous eyes
To Embrace
The Vast, Blissful, Universe
The Irresistible long wait
The Coming and Going
In My Apprehension, to
Forget and Dissolve, to
Unveil the screen Amid
Being in the midst for Millenniums
Was in Aplomb, to
Be one with You, now
You have come as My Consort
As if the outcome of my Penance
Quintessentially in form
Is that in Disguise?
In Flesh and Blood, with
The Warmth of your Body and Heart
The Petrichor emitting from your body
I Snuggled into You
Our bodies Entwined
The Texture of your skin
The Nectar from your lips and tongue
The Essence of the Divine

Compassion on this Terra
Your Voice, Speech and Language
A Celestial Music
Your presence a Fervour, Aroma, Incense
Your Human embrace
Makes me feel
Am no more being Human
In your Being, Infinity and Bliss
I would want to Disembody
I feel Embodied, in
Your Celestial Embrace

❖

Open the Door..I have Come

YOU were here, with
All of us
YOU left for your abode
The day before yesterday, or
Millions of years back, and
Have been in your bliss
All for yourself
I imagine
There, is no sun, moon, stars or galaxies
YOU have perhaps forgotten
Have left here your idols, to see
My father, grandpa, granny, friends and ancestors
Have all left
Have you kept them there?
Have given them a throne
All your Messengers, Saints, Sages, Sufis, Vachanakars and Vedantins
Spake & sung to your glory
The great Scriptures proclaim
That I am ONE and in me
Are all souls, all creatures and living things
For they know not
Death is so near
Suffering no end
Shall again enter into darkness & shall again reborn

My mother, my beloved, my kith & kin & all on this planet
They are all with me to enter our abode
Open the door..I have come

❖

State of Meditation

Meditation in situ

Eyelids drop curtain
Close screen to mundane world
Ears bidding goodbye to outer sounds
Sounds of silence bloom
Bodily attached thoughts renounce
Habitation of bones, blood and nerves cast away
Skin starts sensualising astronomical cool
Terrestrial body consign to oblivion
Realms of inner being manifest
Ubiquity of bliss felt
Self experiences expansion
Encounters universal presence

Meditation Aftermath

Gradually eyes open
World offers to view
Poetry of creation
Sparkle in eyes result
Mark two red wine glasses
Awareness of joy fails to resign
Reminiscences of worldly ties attract
Mind dwindles in dilemma
Forces into the routine
Habitual actions hence take stroll

Nevertheless mind hankers to
Meditate again and again

Meditation Repeats

Retrospective effects compose
Afterthoughts full of joy
Elated mind permits to act
Darkless light offers bliss
Heart centre blossoms
Personality elevates to spiritual vibrations
Knower of knowledge becomes known
Exaltation to formless state
Showers of benedictions occur
Being silent witness to inner and outer worlds
Thus – the Growth, to receive reverence
One of the One merges into – 'the One'

❖

Emotion to Salvation

In the midst of the heart ripping emotion

Words play to create commotion

Even in bright day light pierced by your vision

The long wait showed me direction

Amid all hurt, tears, scar and all the good in motion

Self introspection and rumination lead to determination

Scholarly acquaintances, scriptures, doctrines are exemplification

Knowledge to enlightenment and meditation

Am now on way to salvation

Where is the Present?!

Seconds pass by in their own pace

Illusive past, illusive future present a dream

One dream follows another in fraction of seconds

Unimaginable fraction so fast

Nonsensical mind though perceives it, but in fragments

Tends not to leave its old mannerisms

Avoidable actions accomplish, humans enticed to fall trap

In sensual pleasures of phenomenal world

Life passes in past memory and future anxiety

Unaware days, years roll down sometime after it perceives

Inquiry begins as to – Where is the Present?

Pondering upon, ruminating on and practicing meditation reveals

Longtime after being in the physical world now comprehends – Where is the Present!

❖

Hello! You Both!! Mind! & Body!

My salutations to your friendship
you both, have been such good friends
anybody, for that matter would appreciate and applause.

Having been my guests all through
been so close to each other
you act, like as if you are the big hosts.

You work by the seconds
make know of your after effects to one another
bring happiness and sorrow to each other.

You are more concerned, of your own self
having to reside in me,
shown all causations of pleasure and pain.

All through you have been doing and acting your ways
having not cared, what shall be
repercussions on me.

Over a period, you caused stress, strain
invite certain diseases and mental problems
aren't you not fed up?

Now, I have come to know, that
I have been taken for a ride by you both
this will not do, henceforth.

I now want, you to listen to me
you have not heard of Meditation and Mindfulness
I now teach you, some lessons on that.

I pray, you obey me
as I am giving you both the conducive atmosphere
you needn't worry, I go by your ways to mend.

Oh! Body, you are constructed of the five great elements
you mind, you are made of space and wind
therefore, are such your acts.

In the present moment
this is what you are to do
keep away past, think not of future, strictly.

Enough of wandering
in the mundane world
find solitude, that shall bring joy.

Realise! Who you are
you are not what you were a second back
you inhere within me.

Therefore, practice the methods of meditation
mindfulness is what shall bring you into the path
freedom is what shall be achieved.

I am the source of your existence
derivation of joy is from me
I am the bliss.

After death I get rid of you,
shall leave the planet

who knows, if I shall get you both back.

Now is the time to know,
cleanse, yourselves to capture back
the kingdom of silence, in which is all and complete.

Mind karma, gather blessings, seek the Master
change is what is needed, balance and transform
Hello! You Both!! Mind! & Body!

❖

Time Waits

Time waits since conception in mother's womb

Who knows from how many lives and what karma

Offspring appears into mysterious world again

Life in the womb of time wanders and whirls

Life purpose unknowing, engrossed in mundane humdrum

Incompetence plays role; puzzled steps; life gets baffled

Time alerts, rings warning bells time and again

Wakes-up from slumber of materialistic worldly epidemic

Time is witnesseth, knows all in and out

Time waits none, universal belief

Time waits life to free from it's own womb

Time waits life release into timeless realms

Time waits to offer eternal bliss

The Gods

Have the Gods brought
You on earth?
Were the Gods present while
You took birth?
Are the Gods still there and
You are around them?
Had the Gods planned
You what are?
I am in Love
with you
In return
You have been compassionate
in love with Me
Please wait, I am bit busy
Trying to find
the Gods
I am scared
the Gods
may take you away from Me
I am trying to send
the Gods
Make them intoxicated
into their own divinity to
leave us both alone
in a place where

no time no ageing
For I want You
not to part with Me
We would escape from
the Gods
Enduring stopped
in everlasting immortality like
the Gods
Me and You
Be together in eternity as
the Gods

❖

GOD Met Me (series) Part 1

Vibrant body, light in brilliance coming my way

Furious like a storm, angelic perception emerged to meet

Puzzled appearance caused arduous task of knowing what

In the form, gauging enormous things, in awe of their presence

Surveillance suggest, specify of a king, a beggar, a beautiful woman, an ugly man, landscape of nature and a mini universe

Close quartered looks, in aghast came the query – Who are you?

I am GOD – the voice in high and low decibels of sound to make as if the universe to listen

Stunned when heard, further requests came answers – Am the formless now in form

In amazement of a perception, of a miracle and a revelation, inquiry inevitable from me

Thus the sweet voice: My Lad! Am the Master – The Almighty as your world addresses, have come to meet you

Me in full tears, clasped and enveloped into, being cuddled

GOD Met Me (series) Part 2

Furthermore the cherished, melodious utterance echoed – I Love You and I know You Love Me too

Inquest tickled, long awaited aspiration, troubled 'how' and 'why' of this creation, I beseeched to Him

Tribulation of the world is a trial, He reverts back

When and how to understand, fountain like came my words, to seek

Inquires He, who you think you are

In dismay and astonishment I was in dilemma as to what

You think you have an inner voice – speaks to you now and then- roars the voice

Readily came the answer explicitly in affirmation –Yes!

Existence before you, assimilate to know

You are the master – enlighten!

GOD Met Me (series) Part 3

I have not seen, heard or read of You meeting anyone
False My Lad! He answers – I meet – They do not understand
Formless though, I am in different forms
All that has a form has a name, in them I dwell
O I see, now I know, You are Known, Knower and Knowledge
You caught it right – Ruminate! My Dear!!!
The outer world attracts the senses, thereby to divert
Look into inner self, thereby shall find joy, bliss and peace
You are neither the body nor the senses or the mind
Be a witness to everything, thus shall realise – 'Thou art That' – 'Tat Tvam Asi', You in Me, Me in You
In full tears I kept seeing the luminous light drifting away in the sky

Simple & Simply

It is a Simple Thought
Simply Think
You are not the Simple One
Its Simple,that
You Simply " Thou art That "
They have said in Simple Words
We have to Simply Understand
Sounds Simply Simple, yet
Not as Simple, Simply

Representing Life

Deep in the dark clouds
Birds enjoy flying in the showers of rains
Deep in green forests
Animals, creatures enjoy being there all for themselves
Deep in ocean waters
Fish, aquatic creatures enjoy the 'swim' like no others
Deep in the concrete jungle, villages and mountains
Humans enjoy being in their routine
All represent life to be lived once though and more again and again

❖

Mind-Inner Sunshine

Mind the inner sunshine
Sun the outer
They have brighter and hazy moments
Both covered by their own dark clouds
Once they get cleared
They glow and outshine

04 Nature offers for Us

NATURE SPRINKLES COLOURS

To the Sky
On the Land
In the Water
CAMERA SNATCHES THOSE COLOURS
Adding more to the Original
Beholds them into its Domain
With all its Pride
WE DO SEE THE COLOURS
Reminiscences Hidden
Times Recalled
Now and Then
&
LIFE TO ENJOY

Yes! I am Life

I am as Fresh and Immaculate always
You can't even Imagine
My Pristine Beauty and Importance
I am Freely Available All over
Involuntary You take Me In and Out
You Enjoy My Effect
On your Face, Skin and Body
Your Mind gets Doubly Happy
You gave me the title Cool Breeze
You throw your Dust, Impurities into Me
Make me Impure and Unhealthy
You blame it on Me
Address Me as Pollution
You fill your Tyres
Compress Me to your Benefits
Run Your Machines
I keep the World on the Move
You call Air
Sell with no Gratitude
You Spend to Breathe Me
Go far off places
Resorts, Hill Stations, Beeches and the like
There you Feel
I am there for You
You shower Blessings upon Me
In the language of Yoga

They Proclaim it as Prana
The Life giver
You don't Care
To take Care of Me
Other Creatures and Living Things depend on Me
I am Off from Here
You and Everything is Finished
Existence put to Question
Beware! To see Me, I am there
Yes! I am life

❖

Oh You! World. Now! You Envy

Oh You! World
I was after you
Such love you know
What you gave Me
Hate, Shame, Displeasure, Depression
You want me to give the List
Better you not ask
As it goes endless
You showed your Charm
To Hanker for Money and Power
I shun you
Have now been living beneath a tree
Beside a musical stream
Among the chirping song of the birds
Animals, Insects, Beasts come to me
Both free of fear
We love each other
I understand their language
So do they mine
Hunger and craving has disappeared
I give them nothing
As here in the forest
I do not have anything to give
I only have Love
In return I receive by the bundles
Being among the stars, sunset, sunrise and darkless nights

In the soundless blossoming of the flowers
I live in the ecstasy of nature
What more bliss do I need
I am now the universe
The whole of existence
It loves me
I love it
I am away from You
Oh You! World
Now! You Envy

❖

In The Silence of Forests and Oceans

Life manifested forms time immemorial

Nature's appearance seems quietude

Glimpses establish Ken

Close looks substantiate life in gear

Colossal energy ubiquitous

Animals, Plants, Creatures and Aquatic life living since then

Cheerful, Ecstatic, Joyous in their own sphere

Demonstrating life and death insignificant

Humans adopted change compulsive

Intelligence being foremost free to administer

Holocaust of other lives to their mission of civilized society

Sabotaged perception of their own consciousness

Have human minds turned inarticulate?

Isn't it not late to comprehend?

Recognising significance of other life styles

End of ignorance lights up boundless visionary path

Existence so expansive to perceive ones of the ONE
In the silence of forests and oceans

❖

The River and Me

Somewhere Somehow The River takes birth on Earth
I too born in one part of Earth
As the flow continues more & more water collects
As I grew more & more experience collects
River crosses through mountains, terrains, forests, cities, villages
I cross through emotions, feelings, compassions, setbacks, people as body ages
The River journey feeds across, gives life, it enjoys
My journey goes on, feeding family, workers, paying taxes and interests, I enjoy
It just flows, no flowing back, ends up in vast Ocean
I came through, no looking back, end up in death in vast Endless Infinity

❖

Oh! Human!!!

Oh! Human!!!
You want to kill me
Having used me so Much
I still want to Live
Could You allow Me to
And if You could allow Me to
I could still give You Shade & Comfort
I beautify your World
And don't I satisfy your Hunger
I shall be Home to so many Creatures & Birds
You think only of your Home
You kill me
Let still Peace shower on You
Do not kill Me
Oh! human!!!

Birds Life Style

Sound of chirping birds alarm to wake

Enjoy flight moving place to place

Seeking for food from the sky

Dawn to dusk work hard to fill belly

Every bird healthy no emotions no obesity

Sunset time to go home

Sleep well for the night no insomnia or the sort

One day out of scene not even a trace

Birds' life style exemplary to humans

❖

Like Tree....I too

Like the tree branches look
to reach sky Up

Like pleasant cool breeze shaking leaves in harmony
to say as if I am coming Up

Like this whole scenario seems
to laugh and smile at earth from Up

Like the tree, baby spreads arms and waves
to call it's father to carry and lift Up

Like the secret desire it is bound
to approach better heights Up

Like the tree, I too secretly desire so
to be one into the sky Up

Seconds of Happiness

Like a Woodpecker hitting at the Glass
Calling for my attention as I Pass

Grabbing it from that wicked Hand
Clasped it tight in my Hand

Eyes dwindling in Fear
Accelerated heart beats I couldn't Bear

Holding it in Rescue
Throwing in air it Flew

Sigh of relief; patting its wings like never Before
Like a Roller Coaster ride, I never had Before

Except planet earth a place where can it Find
I Ponder, why can't we be Kind

The Pigeon enjoyed seconds of Happiness
I too enjoyed seconds of Happiness

05 Social

I Know You Are the Soul. But.....!

She conceived again
You gave her kisses
I was still not born
You were so happy
As I came into this world
You took me here and there
I grew so fast
You were proud of me
Introduced me to this world
You were treasure of Joy and Love
You distributed it like a fool
They took it like mad
It never became empty
You did give so much
To all who came your way
You left your body
For me to search you
Where shall I
How shall I
When shall I
Find to meet you again
I know you are the soul

But you left me behind in this world

.......Oh! My Dad!!!

BUT....!

❖

Firsts and Lasts among No Blood Relation

First steps out home world set to offer experience
Kickoff to learning and schooling in coeducation setup
Amazed to see kids all over whom I too was
Embracing first moves of friendship, love and compassion
Growing physically, mentally seemed inevitable
During play laughs, fights where compulsion
Primary finished filtered went higher
High school place of most mischievousness, learning
Entering college, life was wonderful world
Youngsters from different backgrounds and languages
Laugh and fun was astonishing, existence awesome
After pass-out all friends divurge to earn bread and livelihood
Arrived various from vocations, careers and businesses
No trace of most only most loveable remained some time
All gave enough love, affection appeared to be till last
Most left to their abodes leaving fine memories
Last of friends today are on phone
Balancing the outer and inner worlds is bliss and the Now

The Shining Rock

Shining Rock One Of The Many On Earth Rarely Found
Lying Bizarre On The Planet Like Many Other Stones
Creating Under-Worlds Crime Corruption Unlawful People's World
Lives Spent To Maketh Shine By Light
Priced So High Affording The Rich
Making Beloveds Happy Their Own
Beautiful On Damsel's Neck
Blood Lives Sacrificed
Tongues Spell
Diamond

Who Are You?

You have bee

n coming and going

Yes! Since I was a Child

You show me what I want

Sometimes what I don't

Even sometimes horrifying scenes

I see my own self in varied circumstances

It makes me feel happy & enjoy

It makes me feel bad & sorrowful

You know of all things I think & do

You know even my secrets

Hidden in a corner of my Heart

You make them manifested

Are they Real?

Yes! They are, when I keep seeing them

Suddenly they vanish

Are they any stories?

Half told & incomplete

Switching from one scene to the other

With no connection to each other

Bringing all into confusion

Every morning to Get Up & feel

Who are You?

Oh! You are my Dream!!!

Advertisements

I Do Not Pose

do not Pose

Neither I want to Impose

In the faith I Depose

Of the World, there is lot to Expose

The Knowledge, shall be incredible, I Suppose

Of the these things I keep in Repose

For there is no way to Dispose

Resistance to these thoughts, I Oppose

These words, for me and you I Compose

You Are The Lad!

You are the Lad!
Of Your Mother
Of Your Motherland!
Your Father, Sister, Brother, Friend everyone wait
To see you again
Back in form, since
Why and When You left
Carrying gun on shoulders
Have killed fellowmen
You think have place in heaven
You think to fight for a cause
You think are the greatest
Brain Washed, Controlled, Tied up
Life is not what you lead
Dropped in Falsehood & Fanaticism, Understand
Dragged into Terror & Terrorism, Burdened
No heaven up there
Come live free with us here
Comprehend Past, Listen Now
Worst is Future
Oh My Terrorist Brother
Love is what you expect
Far behind is respect

Here you are a suspect

You are the Lad!

Of Your Mother!

Of Your Motherland!

Admission, Apology, Confession Remains

Ask for Forgiveness, Excuse, Concession

Here is your sojourn, come

You are the Lad!

Of Your Mother!

Of Your Motherland!

A Loveable Lady

Desirable Lady many aspire
Blessed in possession feather in cap
Hold her in arms tight
Dream come true to embrace
Kiss her in public with pride
She is epitome of creativity
Performance criteria to earn
Sincere efforts of creation mandatory
Her admiration goes worldwide
Applause received to have clasped

Recipient's karma phenomenal
In field one dreams of the beloved
The Loveable Filmfare's Black Lady Award

Instances in Time

"An important Instance in Time becomes History

At Times there are discussions on History which remain only Instances"

❖

Dishoom! Dishoom!!

In the Movies

Men fight Fisty! Fisty!!

Money & Women are the reason

Stories blended for Entertainment! Entertainment!!

Good Girls! Bad Boys!! Vice versa

Come See! Go See!!

Dishoom! Dishoom!!

Fast & Furious, Mad Max

Speed! Speed!!

All-over Love! Love!!

Thrilling! Thrilling!!

One shot, goes down Whirling! Whirling!!

Gets up, to take another, as fresh Flowering! Flowering!!

Dishoom! Dishoom!!

First came costume predominant Mythological, monumental Historical, then came on the horses Cow Boys

Movie reels rolled and showed man and woman Love Stories, ticklish Cartoons, guns & bombs World Wars

Raising eyebrows Science Fiction, frightening Horrors

Embraces, Dances Kisses! Kisses!!

Kungfu style Fights! Fights!!

Holding seats Tight! Tight!!

Dishoom! Dishoom!!

Early Memories

Early morning found myself full awake

Memories of early childhood coming like slides

How we used to play those penniless games

Rushing to the nearby playground no sooner from school

Mothers finding all kids in the ground or neighbour's compound

Shouting at them after late evening to bring them back home

Only our bodies were the investment to play

At the most we would require a stick, one or two marbles or a piece of round stone

Rest would be our most strong legs and hands and cheerful minds

In the games continuous laughs and small fights were must which we would have them again and again

Striking deals with skillful marble players at times for buying old marbles from, for just two or three pennies

Most strong and skilled ones would win games but no regrets for who lost

Those were the days to cherish, shall remain early memories

A Big Lie

"A 'Big Lie' uttered, demands in response an expertise to utter several more.

Some try to expertise and keep enjoying the act, ultimately fall prey to the lie"

❖

क्या बात है दोस्त

वाह! क्या बात है दोस्त आखिर तेरी खबर आई
इधर सदियां बीत गई इंतज़ार में ही
तैयारी तो हमारे जनाज़े की हो रही थी
निकल पड़े हम ज़िंदा तेरे खबर आते ही।

Alas! Oh My Friend!

Alas! Oh My Friend! At last your message has arrived
Here an era has passed by waiting
Preparation of my funeral procession was going on
I came back from dead as soon as your message came

❖

यार सूरज

यार सूरज! मैं भी देख रहा हूँ, जब से मैं छोटा था

तुम तो रोज़ उदय होते हो, डूबते हो,

तुमने कभी विराम ली है?

बस कह डालते हैं कि तुम आते हो, जाते हो

यूँ तो तुम्हारा कभी सूर्योदय, सूर्यास्त हुआ ही नहीं

ख्याल करेंगे तुम अगर एक पल भी विराम करोगे

क्या होगी हमारी हालत, पक्षी, मछली, समुद्री जीवों की, पेड़-पौधों की

तुम ऐसा नहीं कर सकते, क्योंकि तुम अपने यार हो

सूर्या नारायण हो

तुम्हें हम सबकी तरफ से शुक्रिया, नमस्तुतः

Ohhh My Friend Sun!

Ooh Friend Sun! I am seeing you since I was a child

Everyday you come up and go down

Have you ever taken rest?

We keep telling you just come and just go

Actually there is no Sunrise and Sunset

Let us think for a while if you take rest

What will be of us Humans, Birds, Animals, Fish, Aqua Ocean life and Plants and Trees?

You cannot do so because You are My Friend You See!

You are the Sun God Narayan!

Thanks to You on behalf of All of us Namostute!

❖

ये मालूम नहीं था

बुढ़ापा कितना भयानक है, ये मालूम नहीं था
अपने मंसूबे को हिला देगी, ये मालूम नहीं था
अपने दोस्त भी दूर हो जायेंगे, ये मालूम नहीं था
सब जिगर के टुकड़े अलग होंगे, ये मालूम नहीं था
चेहरे पे रौनक आहिस्ता-आहिस्ता घट जायेगी, ये मालूम नहीं था
कुछ इस तरह तन्हाई में ज़िंदगी गुज़र जायेगी, ये मालूम नहीं था।

I Didn't Know

Old age is so horrifying, I didn't know
My mind set is shaken by, I didn't know
My friends would go far away, I didn't know
All relations close to heart have moved away, I didn't know
Brightness on the face slowly diminishes, I didn't know
In aloneness life shall pass by, I didn't know

❖

06 Music

Music

Silence of Eternity breaks into Infinitude
Nature salutes, offers conducive climate
Love Hearts meet, Broken Hearts heal
Hearing, Love enhances
Goosebumps result
Birds, Animals, Trees turn attention towards
All senses become Ear
All body joints activate to
Start a full-fledged Dance
Vocal cords vibrate creating Musical chords
Blown air transmutes Atmosphere, Ambience, Aura
Percussionist spills life from dead skin
Hands as if trembling to procreate
Finger tips play on strings to generate
Notes, Tunes
Rhymes, Rhythm, Pitch, Bass
Poets' lyrics, emotions, imagination
Unfold, Augment into Melody
Bamboo, Drums, Pipe, Plates, Fruit Carcass, Mud Pots, Strings, Sticks
Aid to Musicality
Artists, Music Instruments form the choir
Respecting the hymn

Language barrier eliminate

Soul tunes manifest

Country borders erased

Presentation to world

Music

❖

07 Rhymes for Children and Adults

Jumping Jumping Went to School

Morning, morning saw outside
Everything looks fresh, fresh, green, green
Felt to take long, long breaths
Want to be as fresh
Brush in mouth up & down, sideways
Sprinkled water to the face
Mummy calls to have some milk
Glimpses from the window
Birds chirping, hopping, hopping, tree to tree
Wondering, wondering where do they go
Questioning myself, do they have a school too?
Yells Mummy to have bath & breakfast
Oh! Mummy! Mummy!! Coming, coming
Jumping, jumping went to school

❖

Chukku! Bukku!! Chukku! Bukku!!

Chukku! Bukku!! came to town
People rushing to see train
Some buy tickets to go around
Station Master whistles – 3
Bell Rings 1 – Train at platform
Bell Rings 2 – Shall leave in few minutes
Bell Rings 3 – Shall leave in a minute
Chukku! Bukku!! Chukku! Bukku!!

Engine Driver Super Strong
Putting coal in fire
Though sweating shall not stop
Shhhhh sounds driver
Shhhhh sounds steam engine
Iron wheels revolve on rail,
Towns and cities, farms and forests passed over
Chukku! Bukku!! Chukku! Bukku!!

Place to place decades passed by
Whistles and horns of train
Set time for the world
Carried goods by the tons
People commuted to earn bread
Happy travellers saw world
Millions and Billions Miles it went
Chukku! Bukku!! Chukku! Bukku!!

Child on back, elders crawling, to imitate train
Entertained kith and kin
Oh! Now a rare sight
Sighting train happy children
Jumping on toes, counting bogies
Bye! Bye!! On platforms was for some
Parting life forever, now a bygone story
Chukku! Bukku!! Chukku! Bukku!!

Diesel engines arrive at stations, go in subways
Electric trains, Bullet Trains replace show
Less sound, more fast, pace of life super fast
Hurry and worry take the toll
Cheerful journeys down memory lane
Like all obsolete now in museum
Poor Chukku! Bukku!! Great Chukku! Bukku!!
Chukku! Bukku!! Chukku! Bukku!! Chukku! Bukku!!...

❖

Hi! Hippy!! I am a Gypsy!!!

Hi Hippy!
Hippie! Hippie!!
I am not a Hippy!
You are not a Hippy!
Gypsy! Gypsy!! Hi! Hi!!
I am a Gypsy!
You are a Gypsy!
Whole World Gypsy! Gypsy!!

Go around Wander! Wander!!
Play music Boogie! Woogie!!
Spirits be Frisky! Frisky!!
Searching Browsing Google! Google!!
Download Upload Apps! Apps!!
Stomach full Giggle! Giggle!!

Hi! Hippy!! I am a Gypsy!!!
Hi! Hippy!! I am a Gypsy!!!
Hi! Hippy!! I am a Gypsy!!!

❖

Zappy Zappy Guy Happy Happy Gal

Who is Nutty Nutty
Everyone says Not Not
By the Naughty Naughty
Now are all Taught Taught
Hustle and Bustle of town
Crossing Bumpy Bumpy roads
Putting in Jumpy Jumpy state
Having no Shackle Shackle
So one Crackle Crackle
Zappy Zappy guy
Happy Happy gal

Jumping Jumping on the Mattress

Jumping Jumping on the mattress
Hitting Hitting getting hit by the pillow
Going Going around the house
Playing Playing hide & seek
Enjoying Enjoying holidays with siblings
Having Having no past no future
Laughing Laughing stomach full Now
Hahaha! Hahaha!! Hahaha!!!

Children always live in the Now. They exhibit inner joy and bliss. As time passes by they get attached to all sorts of relationships and worldly matters. Thereby creating a trivial past and dreaming of a bombastic future. So, as man grows he slowly forgets living in the Now.

I personally feel animals and birds live in the Now and therefore have formed a unique life way of living. It seems they enjoy life more than we humans.

Hello! Lately I have bought a new mattress, thinking that it would give some comfort to my back. It seems to say to me, to live in the Now.

Remembering childhood days of jumping, hitting and playing on mattress made me write this post. Hope you All enjoy as much as we did.....

Hahaha!!!

❖

End...

Comments from My Blog

I have received some very Good and Beautiful Comments on my Blog Posts which I would want to share a few of them here, so as to the reader would get an idea of what others think. Actually there are some more than 6000 comments but I am sharing very important few. I thank all of them from the bottom of my heart to have given the boost to write well and also inspired me to write more and more since the inception of my Blog. I give here the address for my Blog, whosoever wants can go there and browse. Thanks

www.theshivasponder.wordpress.com

On My About

C Niranjan

Anna,

I liked your recent article titled 'in pursuit of business'. Your views that the world can not do without business reminds me Basavanna's 'Kaayakave Kailasa'. While your views that the whole world is interdependent reminds me of Buddha's teaching of 'Pratityasamutpada' which translates to 'dependent origination'.

It is a sheer joy reading your blog where Buddha and Basava transcend in the latest form!

Niranjan Cholayya

Itihas Sarwade

Hello uncle,

First of all thanks 2 myth!! I do really admire you for your fascinating articles, this blog shows that how the human race being evolved with racism and thank u for the tips for keeping the skin healthy, i wanna share this wonderful article with my friends also, thank you uncle for this article , keep writing much more article and inspire us!! you are our great mentor!

thank u

itihas

multitudeofmythoughts

I would like to answer here rather than on my blog,that what makes me say you are a multi talented person. First is your career wise achievements in diversified fields, second is this versatile blog which gives information on various topics throwing light on your knowledge in various subjects. Moreover this about page and the matter on other links speak up everything about you.

atrangizindagieksafar

Everything I said Shiva is the truth... those who read your blogs know that I an speaking nothing but the truth. I kept wondering about the gifs then hunted for these... knew YOU'll be able to connect with them more. Believe me... it was a real pleasure making this for you.... I enjoyed it every bit. Especially because I kind of knew you'd taste. Sending a big smile and a hug your way. Always be happy.

The Soulcentric Shivangi

Wish you a very very Happy Birthday sir!:-)

May you keep lightening others with you charismatic aura and May God bless you with his grace..

Where is the party sir...I am waiting for the treat!!!!!

Avid Observer

Your blog is filed with inspiration. I loved the poetry section. You portray really deep thoughts through your words. Your thoughts are enlightening

On State of Meditation

HEMA SUBRAMANIAM

Shiva,

You are a philosopher n a poet..one of the rarest n blessed combinations. A everyday ritual so beautifully put across.

For me meditation gave me a kind of different strength, a kind of spiritual calmness (am not much of a spiritual person),a kind of joy!!

You delve deep into the root of your subjects n that fascinates me!!.

Thank you very much for yet another scintillating piece.

Deb Cowdrey

Awe thanks Shiva for your very kind words!! I love all your knowledge and insight that you share with us...you know so much in these matters as you have explained before. I know that we are learning about this from one who really knows of these things. I hope more people will begin to meditate too...it would do the world a whole lot of good!! Thank you for your New Year wishes and I too wish you much bliss, happiness and abundance in 2018!!

Happy Meditative Hugs,

Deb

Miriam (Delphini 510)

Thank you Shiva for this positive and calm post. Meditation silences the chattering of ones mind and the outside and clears your spirit. I do practice it but have not been regular enough lately. Walking meditation is one that always is with me though.

Will heed your thoughts.

Have a happy and fulfilling year Shiva

Miriam

On: Chukku Bukku Chukku Bukku

Marta of Moments

Beautiful tribute to a disappeared train. In our country it used to be like this too. Now everyone is looking at their smartphones, so is our individualistic society, as the second picture of your post shows. It is a global phenomenon in today's world. I agree with you: everything goes too fast and, therefore, there is no pause for reflection, real thinking. Just consummerism and constant update, living in permanent anticipation of future as current philosophers say. I love the onomatopoeic words in your poem as they follow the sounds of the train. In the first stanza the three "Bell rings!" capture the same tempo of the train stops. In the second stanza the "shhhhh sounds" reproduce exactly what happens when the train is running. This is nice too: "Millions and Billions Miles it went". The double rhyme adds rhythm to the poem followed by the repetitive onomatopoeia closing each stanza. The increasing onomatopoeic repetitions of the last stanza reinforce the value of that train. I like this poem very much.

Cornelia of corneliaweberphotography

Shiva, what a brilliant post, thank you so much for sharing. As a child in Germany I lived right next to the railways, back than coal engines, I used to wave at the conductors getting back a hunk and waving hands. At our house there used to be the stop for the train to reload the engine with coals, this was really fascinating for me to watch and to listen to the chatter of all workers, especially at night all that commotions would wake me up. I have taken the train in many different countries of the world. The most impressive I remember in Sri Lanka like 30 some years ago, sitting across this family brining out their food they shared with laughter and happiness. Their little daughter with the most beautiful eyes, communicating with her with hands and eyes, shared with me that she never had a doll in her life.

Exchanging addresses with her parents , as I got back home, I got a sweet doll and mailed it off to her. So riding a train can bring happiness.

Deb Cowdrey

Oh Shiva, this is fantastic. Yes I have ridden on a Chukku! Bukku! a few times. You have really captured the life and essence of trains gone past. You are right about how today it's so individualized, everyone busy on their phones and computers. In some ways technology has done a disservice to communication, rather than enhancing it. Love thd pics too!

Choo Choo hugs,

Deb

LDG luciledegodoy

Very enjoyable reading a thoughtful post. Thanks for reminding us all of the distracting lifestyle, senselessly adopted by many, who prefer to watch smartphones than to mingle with other people. I guess you meant the same happens on WP with those running from post to post to 'like' and never interacting with anyone. I concur with your thoughts.

Thanks.

Comments on Blog Post Where is the Present

Annika Perry

Shiva, powerful thoughts about the illusive present … more than ever people around the globe are seeking mindfulness to capture the present, but in the process are often too concentrated, busy to notice its presence. An important post, and interesting video by Deepak Chopra

On: Birds Lifg Style

Erika

How I miss the birds' songs during the winter season, and how much more do I appreciate them again. Beautiful creatures that bring so much joy.

Pramod Puri

Well, expressed. But that 'life style examplary to human" is being destroyed by the wars like the one in Ukraine. The plight of birds does not appear on the screen.

On: Concrete Jungle Night

KK

This is a real poem. Comparison is so real and true.

Swami Yesudas

"Unlike humans, animals, birds in peaceful hours get energised for tomorrow

Some for some best dreams may come true and is good during late hours

Shame on humans, make night conducive for improper, illegal activities

Human engaged always takes lot from nature gives back crap."

On: Your Arms Like Octopusy Tentacles

Cornelia of corneliaweberphotography

Shiva, that is just a beautiful love poem, filled with all compassion and desire for lovers to become one in the physical world. Yet myself I take it as a spiritual message to become ONE with the source of TRUTH, emerging my soul in compassion.

Shivangi

Lovely poem Shiva. Yours is an original style! Inimitable!

Marta of Moments

Very beautiful and sensual. I like the initial surprising effect of the title and the first two lines, where my immediate reaction was getting a feeling of oppression, as if choking, because of the "octopussy tentacles" and "griped me". However, the following two verses change this feeling completely and turn the meaning of the poem into something pleasurable and emotionally intense: "Unaware of facts of love/ stunned to see myself in goosebumps". At this point the imagery becomes very beautiful. Love this: "Intimacy to the core of fondness/ magic of fascination turns into inflorescence." The next coming lines suggest a most lovely mixture of carnal and spiritual love at the same time. Great poem!

Patty

I know you have written more poetry in the past, but this on has a different feel to it.

You remind me of a Dutch phrase 'Still waters have deep grounds'. Meaning; silent (introvert, quite) people possess profound thoughts.

Enjoy your weekend, I will be dancing a three-day festival ☺

On:Jumping Jumping on the Mattress

Anika Perry

Shiva, this is a wonderful poem caputuring the fun of childhood through the repititions at the start mimicing the actions, reinforing the joy as well as lending a light child-like quality to the words. Ahh..this brought back great memories of jumping on beds, playing 'pirates' around the house and recreating this play with my son when he was young! (Although I refrained from jumping on the bed but always up for a pillow fight!)

Suzanne of patriciaruthsusan

Enjoyable post, Shiva. I try to live in the moment but it's difficult for an adult. I keep trying though. ☺ *— Suzanne*

Anika Perry

Shiva, this is a wonderful poem caputuring the fun of childhood through the repititions at the start mimicing the actions, reinforing the joy as well as lending a light child-like quality to the words. Ahh..this brought back great memories of jumping on beds, playing 'pirates' around the house and recreating this play with my son when he was young! (Although I refrained from jumping on the bed but always up for a pillow fight!)

On: State of Meditation

HEMA SUBRAMANIAM

Shiva,

You are a philosopher n a poet..one of the rarest n blessed combinations. A everyday ritual so beautifully put across.

For me meditation gave me a kind of different strength,a kind of spiritual calmness (am not much of a spiritual person),a kind of joy!!

You delve deep into the root of your subjects n that fascinates me!!.

Thank you very much for yet another scintillating piece.

Shivangi

What a lovely poetry and so many lovely reactions and comments Shiva. Do send this one to Spirit poetry contest, I am sure it will be a winner.

Deb

Awe thanks Shiva for your very kind words!! I love all your knowledge and insight that you share with us...you know so much in these matters as you have explained before. I know that we are learning about this from one who really knows of these things. I hope more people will begin to meditate too...it would do the world a whole lot of good!! Thank you for your New Year wishes and I too wish you much bliss, happiness and abundance in 2018!!

Happy Meditative Hugs,

Deb

xo

Thoughtsnlifeblog

Wow you have loads of comments on this post. I loved it and the first two phases made me laugh because thats quite true. It is only when regularily meditate daily can we feel the magic, the freedom and clarity. Well written your point is made.

EttaD

Thank you so much Shiva! After reading your post today, I made the decision to step away from my desk to take 15 minutes to do absolutely nothing! It was a form of meditation for me to block out the world and appreciate my surroundings for those few minutes! Thank you!!

xxx

On: Hello! You Both!! Mind! & Body!

Meenakshi Sethi

What a great post Shiva! How simply you tamed both naughty, tantrum throwing kids. We all need to live that way. I guess it should be taught in school to little nurturing minds, How to control and live life in a more appropriate way.

Bethbyrnes

Shiva, this reminds me of the many enlightened masters I have studied from Krishnamurti to Meher Baba to Rajneesh. It is so important to reflect on the collaboration between mind and body and to help them support each other. A poem is a lovely way to communicate this concept. So soothing, too.

Infinite Living

A very beautiful profound poetry. Indeed we are taken for a ride by this duo, until awareness kicks in and we can some conscious choices.

On: Emotion to Salvation

Meenakshi Sethi

You are generous soul who knows how to make others smile ☺

I wish I could inspire you to write something big one day. It will be honour .

Thank You!

Gail of Snapshotsincursive

Your words have lightened the portal. Thank you, Shiva.

Kamal of boundlessblessingsblog

Splendid lines of emotion and how it leads to salvation, Shiva. Loved the perfect picture of an eagle soaring to freedom. Radhika is a wonderful blogger too. Thanks for the awesome poem of perfection.

Clare

These words are packed with Truth.I loved this — especially– "Scholarly acquaintances, scriptures, doctrines are exemplification" In deed, we are all headed towards the realization of freedom or, salvation. I wrote something similar "The Salvific Power of Work" yesterday you might like to check it out.Nicely written, Shiva.

On: Jumping Jumping Went to School

Cornelia of corneliaweberphotography

Shiva again you are spreading JOY, thank you. As my photography includes school photography and when I ask children what they want to be in the future, I get such wonderful responses. I admire children's imagination, they feel like they can do anything and that's the way it should be.

Deb Cowdrey

I think there is much that we can learn from children. I think we lose that innocence and imagination as we grow up because "adults" teach us to. I love those who never lose their imagination and who see things differently than as it is. Those are the real teachers of the world! Let's not squelch their desire to be themselves and to have freedom of unique and individual thoughts! I also think we can learn a lot from birds too…let's fly and be free!! Love this post Shiva!!

Hugs,

Deb

xo

Theburning heart

Nothing like teaching children by making the subject fun, like through singing Rhymes

Miriam of delphini510

Wonderful and true post as all of yours are. Children, the biggest responsibility we have so you are so right. They need the environment and the enthusiasm from the adult world to give them a good and nourishing place to grow.

Miriam

Ben Aqiba

Hello Shiva, lovely post with my favorite sort of people.Kids 🙂 Thank you

<u>On: Dishoom Dishoom</u>

Moushmi Radhanpara

Yes, I did enjoy reading this, as I enjoy the Dishoom and the thug there.

A brilliant write up.

Success Inspirers' World

A great one. Entertaining, informative, educative, and inspiring all at once. This is our world. Thanks for sharing Shiva!

michnavs

I love the play up of words here Shiva…and the sounds it produced and the imagies it created..making the whole piece very powerful..

radhikasreflection

Haha! This one was a sure movie entertainer Shiva. Went through all the eras along with your words and enjoyed the dishoom n between.

Lovely to read your reply Shiva. When I was small I would think the sound automatically came when the hero bashed the villain. 😆

Why didn't you pursue your dream of becoming an actor?

Dancingpalmtrees

Your post was funny and made me laugh. Brought smiles to my face. Also especially true of American movies. Love action films. My brother Stephen and I are big fans of Super Hero movies based on the comics of our youth. I graduated from high school in 1977 so that the 1970s have special significance for me.

On: Hi! Hippy!! I am a Gypsy!!!

Marta of MOMENTS

Beautifully expressed as always. Again this poem is very onomatopoeic with words repeating themselves, song-like. It matches the rhythm and the picture of the dancing people below. It is essentially a poem of joy, a chant to life, very nice. I like the references to Google and to the digital world. In a way, you are blending our still analogic souls with the inevitable digital era. Great! I still have not found a musician for your lovely "Chukku Bukku!" poem (one of my favorites of yours), but I will ask someone I know. We will see… Patience.

RhapsodyBoheme

Simply beautiful and yes indeed, we are all Gypsies

Kamal of boundlessblessingsblog

Oh you made my heart turn into a gypsy, Shiva. Loved the awesome poem and the presentation was so beautiful, I have no words to say but that we are all gypsies in our lives and want to be free and roam freely where no one dare touch our souls and we can openly free ourselves. Great post.

Deb

DebLol…funny how when you get something in your head sometimes it sticks there all day. I love the image and words too…just wanted to let you know that's all. Happy Singing!!

Oh Shiva what fun that was!! You are right in this modern world we can be Gypsies without evening leaving our home. We can travel anywhere in the world via our phone, laptop, pc, or television. We can learn so much and all we have to do is Google!! It makes me feel tipsy tipsy to be a gypsy!! 😉

Hugsy Wugsy, I too love the words of that Gypsy picture however they are not my own, usually they are but in this instance they are not, but they do resonate with me.

Annette Rochelle Aben

A poet with a gift for using words, to make certain his voice is heard!

Etta D

Hi! Hippy!! I am a Gypsy!!! I've always wanted to be a Gypsy, to sing, dance and wander. Then I got older and realise I didn't have to be a Gypsy to do those things. I love this upbeat Hap-Happy post!!

On: Zappy Zappy Guy Happy Happy Gal

Meenakshi Sethi

Hi Shiva! I'm a teacher and teaching since last 27 years. From the day of last exam of my 12th std. I successfully managed my own prep school before my marriage. Now I'm taking private classess . So students upto 9th std come at my home in evening. They are of all ages starting from 5 years.

They thoroughly enjoyed and repeated few lines and were asking me who wrote it. I showed them your blog

Patty

Love it. We need more of these funny writings in these times full of dark events.

Thank you for bringing a smile around our globe

Prakash Hegade

He he.. This was cute and fun! Zappy Happy!

Deb

Lol awe that does sound like fun!

Wow how about that…who knew such a fun poem would hold such an inner meaning…well you did!!

Yes that would be fun for her to have the higher class sing that. Boy that's impressive that she heads up a school like, good for her!!

Wonderful that you had a chance to visit. Hope your Mom is still on the road to recover.

Hugs,

Deb xo

On: My Ungrateful Life

Anonymous

What a wonderful n great person you are Shiva!

Feeling Grateful is one of the finest virtues of mankind n you have it in abundance! Am glad you shared this with us.Revealed a bit more of your gracious self!

Loved this !!

Happy writing.

On: Big Lie

Subbashini Meenakshi Sundaram

One can be an expert in lying anywhere but not to one's ownself.

Wendy

Oh so very true Shiva! What a web we weave when we lie and in the end we entangle and strangle ourselves in our own web…

jacquelineobyikocha

The thing is when a lie pervades, the original lie gets forgotten and more lies piled on top of it.

Deb

"O, what a tangled web we weave when first we practice to deceive!" ~ Walter Scott

And this isn't from Charlotte's Web!! lol

You could elaborate on this, there are white lies and black lies. Because one is a fib (white lie) does it make it any less of a lie….like when your wife asks you "do I look fat?" and you say no but mean yes…is that ok?

Oh this could be a lot of fun…but in general, as a rule, lies will always track you down!!

What say you Shiva?

Hugs,

Deb

xo 😉

Calmkate

Honesty is the best policy and much easier to remember … those that lie often forget who they told what!

Swamiyesudas

Very Good, my Dear Shiva! We need More reminders like this. …Lies, big or small, make us their prey.

Thanks for the reminder, and Regards.

Corneliaweberphotography

Interesting conversations here, upon your great post, Shiva, which I can't agree more. Just minutes before I read your post, I came across an article of a 91 year old survivor of the Holocaust, who is talking about hate. Before he entered the first of the three concentration camps he had been, his mother whispered in his ear " Be strong and don't let any hate enter your heart. Never forget that love is stronger than hate". Those wise words became his tool of survival. Hating somebody never makes sense. It doesn't change anything that happened nor does it serve the future. Hate makes one weak and diffuses the view for the good. This man had lost his entire family in Auschwitz concentration camp, yet after he was freed 1945 he shared his last piece of bread with a young German mother and child most probably a Nazi, but he didn't care, by hating her would have proofed that he wasn't any better than the Nazis. Why am I sharing this story? Because hate and big lies stem from the same issues, named fear, not facing the truth.

Infinite Living

Lies are such prisons that one builds for oneself! You have touched upon a powerful truth.

Ranjeeta Nath Ghai

True... Satya vachan. One lie leads to another then another... Some people are such compulsive liars that they lie about everything they do

Dancingpalmtrees

The Key word is "practice to deceive." Everyone lies because you don't feel like answering questions or you don't want people to know what's going on in your life. Often I will say I'm fine. I'm okay even when I'm not. Or as a woman you make up a story to get some pesky guy that you're not interested in away from you. Sometimes it's better to lie as not to hurt the guys feelings or prevent some form of violence.

Ben Aqiba

lie is a lie, no matter what kind no matter what the truth hides behind ☺

Keep writing

delphini510

Shiva, you have taken up a very big and interesting occurrence. Why, in the first place are lies – big and small – so common?

I am not talking about political or religious leaders lies. Why so many in everyday life.

There are actually compulsive liers who build their lives on a succession of lies to cover up what would otherwise be just an ordinary? life.

Then we have all the social lies and the so called white lies.

Yes, they snowball, thus covering up the first ones.

Sorry about the length of this answer Shiva.......carried away. ☺

miriam

kishanlakhotia

A liar can never speak a lie to him/her self.

<u>On:GOD Met Me (series) Part 1</u>

Wow Shiva that is beautiful. I love your reason for God coming to you, that made me nod and smile and agree, you are right. Congratulations on your 100th post too!! Perfect subject to celebrate with!!

Hugs,

Deb. ☺

ladycee

Hello dear Shiva, I come across cyberspace to see how you are doing and I do not come empty-handed or with empty mouth.

First, let me congratulate you on your 100th post!

How wonderful that such an occasion highlights your meeting with God. It sounds as if you had a magical, supernatural experience.

God is indeed high yet humble, to search us out and make himself known to us. Thank you for sharing your experience.

Oluwakemi Toluwalase

it's great when God meets with us 👌 *Love your post* ☺

<u>Once in a While</u>

atrangizindagieksafar

Absolutely agree with you 100%. People's attitudes change as per their need of you.... have faced it many times....

On: The Long Wait

corneliaweberphotographer

Dear Shiva, a bit late to respond to your post. Some posts I read again and again to grasp and ponder on the deeper message and yours are one of them. Accepting the concept of life as a circle from birth to death isn't easy at times, yet very much an amazing teaching once we understand it. Suffering pain can easily distract from our purpose of living and being as a physical body on this earth, yet there is so much more to it. Our physical body is just an illusion of our mind, yet it takes awareness to wake up from this and living in gratitude.

dilkiaawazsunoblog

Zindagi ka ek dastoor Hai, Jo aaya wo jaata zaroor Hai. Seekh sake gar hum unse kuch, jee sake khushi ke pal sang Unke. Ek khoobsoorat Yaaden ban fir wo rehta Zindagi bhar zaroor hai.

The people who come into our lives leave their impact in a positive or negative way, better for us to remember the happy things pray for their happiness and let go.. and by this we also grow..

It was a heart touching post.

On: You are the Lad!

Gayatri Sharma

Apt and so well written! A very strong message delivered in a heart touching way!

Deb

Very deep Shiva. My favorite line is… Life is not what you lead. It's ironic that they "think" they are fighting for their cause because they don't like ours. They "think" we are trying to impose on them our way of living and thinking, and they are not going to accept it. But aren't they doing the same thing that they are killing us for? Aren't they trying to impose their beliefs and lifestyle on us? What hypocrites. If they only "got" that, perhaps they would understand and stop. I doubt it though, as you say they are brainwashed! Poor lads, they have such an opportunity here on this beautiful planet and yet they waste it by living their life for someone else. Which goes back to my favorite line...Life is not what you lead

Well said Shiva!!

Deb

joyindestructible

I like this one a lot and a perspective on terrorists I've never heard expressed. Truly, they are our misguided brothers, desperate for something better and deluded into reaching for death to obtain their dream rather than reaching for what they really want, life.

Wendy

Such a sad truth Shiva so eloquently described.

You're absolutely right Shiva... it truly is unimaginable what their parents must go through... Often they have to cope with the tragedy of losing their child and then the horrendous guilt and loss of knowing the suffering their offspring has caused to others...Truly a devastating issue all round... xxx

Aquileana

Powerful message and verses... even more if we keep in mind the circumstances of quite Precarious peace, these days... It seems the world is heading towards a blind alley, somehow.

These verses in particular tyruly resonated with me : " Love is what you expect... Far behind is respect".

True, sigh... I hope there is still light and better days ahead!... Sending best wishes to you, dear Shiva ☆

On: Where shall I be taken? The Quest Remains

Deb

OMG Shiva this is fantastic! It matters not where you are taken as you shall dwell in peace. Where others have gone and been sent is of no concern to you. Do not stay awake at night wondering, hoping for the answer, just be filled with happiness and joy and you will enjoy wherever you are taken. I absolutely love the end "You are here"...genius!! Brilliant post.

Deb

corneliaweberphotography

This is the second time I am reading your post, in order to really understand it with my heart, it is deep and carries out the truth so brilliantly and simply. Than you ever Shiva for sharing your talent and wisdom.

Alok Singhal

Deep thoughts! We are nothing in this universe, yet some of us consider ourselves to be so accomplished.

infinite Living

Love the rhythm and the profoundness of this poem. The picture imprints your words so well!

On: The Greats

HEMA SUBRAMANIAM

ineffable joy experienced reading this Shiva!

loved this!

What an admirable trait you have been ingrained with !!

The way you bring forth n pour the love n affection n gratitude is commendable!

Shows how much you love n respect each individual

These gems are indeed our blessings n sometimes more than a family member.

My dad in law too had a similar situation wherein the maharaj.. the cook was adored by one n all no's given an house in Bangalore n the farm hands are all Lakhpati's,

Can relate to this wholeheartedly.

May we be as humble n grateful as You!!

Stay blessed!!

On: My Ungrateful Life

This is a beautiful post! Many people say there is nothing to be grateful for. The world is full of problems, a dystopia full of fears and impending doom. Your blog post debunks that with a powerful attitude of gratitude!

Gail

I knew "taking a pause" at the end of a busy day would have its rewards. I found them in your post. Blessings.

Erika

It is a shame, a bit shame, that even doesn't meet the core of the tragedy, that food and water are a priviledge to have. And many don't even notice how gifted they are. Let's do our part as good as we can!

I just learned that 40% of the food goes in the trash. It is a shame. To me this is a no-go. In case there are leftovers, they are wrapped and stored for later. But I know that the awareness of this has been rising. By being vegetarian, I want to honor our animal friends and their gifts for us.

HEMA SUBRAMANIAM

What a wonderful n great person you are Shiva!

Feeling Grateful is one of the finest virtues of mankind n you have it in abundance! Am glad you shared this with us.Revealed a bit more of your gracious self!

Loved this !!

Happy writing.

<u>On: On Two Beloveds</u>

HEMA SUBRAMANIAM

Its a Gem of a Poem!

I am intrigued as to how easily n quickly your ever sharp mind n grasp into any form of poetry/poem. In this Diamond... shaped Etheree...Your passion n love for writing n learning is mind boggling! Such a lovely n truthful and blood curling poem brought out so vividly, inviting the green importance in possessing the diamond By Any Means! A true to life Poem brought Alive by You. They always been involved in all Evils!! Such a Beautiful Poem Shiva!

<u>On: Yaar Suraj</u>

HEMA SUBRAMANIAM

We all love the sun n feel blessed that we r given a day more to enjoy life. Your lines made me view The Sun as another important person in my life WOW!!

Only you n the poet in you could have brought out such beautiful lines!

Excellent!!

Rekha Sahay

Beautiful poem and I liked the writing style too. All pics are great Shiva. Suraj viram nahi le sakta kyonki duniya uske saath chal rahi hai. Din aur raat uske saath-saath bandhe hai.

On: Celetial Embrace

HEMA SUBRAMANIAM

Another masterpiece of yours Shiva!It made me ponder over the richness of your thoughts.A simple word made into an exotic n mesmerising poem. You make us soak into the richness of your words , love the imagery you force us into!! A powerful poem.Your emotions are so easy going n flowing into a beautiful n fantastic poem. Keep them coming!!

Wendy

"Your Human embrace, Makes me feel,

Am no more being Human, In your Being, Infinity and Bliss…"

What beautiful words.. How wonderful to have this feeling in life! X

Deb

Embrace the Universe in all its forms and it will embrace you back. Appreciate and learn from all that is out there to teach us in nature, in the heavens, the moon, the stars, the sun…there is so much to learn and love that one lifetime is never enough…we must come back many times to embrace the celestial world!! Love this even more every time I read it…bravo Shiva!!

You are so full of knowledge Shiva, I love that you share it with us. We are very fortunate to be blessed with your writings. Keep them coming and know that they don't depend on others comments to make you happy, your thoughts are what matter. Yes the music is beautiful also.

Such a wonderful request of celestial showers, I won't use my umbrella when they come down!!

Thank you, wishing your Sunday is or was as thoughtful and embracing too!!

Much Love & Light,

Deb

Tony

The mood lifts. Your words help to do that. You say what I know in my heart but it comes from you strongly and with conviction! Thanks Shiva. Another poem this morning … the good friends on WordPress are become my teachers!!… tells me to let go of grudges. There's the rub.

Erika Kind

Reading your poem was a celestial experience. True love when all becomes one!

Pranabaxom

Shiva, this is a beautiful and deeply thoughtful poem. I was looking at the crescent moon on the accompanying image and thinking about Lord Shiva and Sati.

Soumya

Reading this was like a watching a preview of a movie.. here The transition is brilliant while maintaining the same flow . It requires a certain degree of finesse. Excellently executed piece…

On: Sorrow ---Most Private Affair

Maniparna Sengupta Majumder

WE can't share our personal sorrows all the time.

"All only for themselves

Would not want to show the world Living life's journey In their own Music" So beautifully said…

Heartafire

Indeed! It is good to see you in such good form, lovely poetry!

Fourth Generation Farmgirl

Shiva, you are always so kind and generous with your beautiful and uplifting words! Thank you very much for taking time to read my blog as well as visit and follow "Almost Farmgirl." It is a delight to hear from you and know that you enjoyed my posts! Many, many thanks for your lovely comment. Take care! 😊 *xo*

Lady G

Wow, there is so much truth here. We all have a particular sorrow that is very private; one we never want to share.

Heartfelt, eloquent and thought-provoking.

I loved it

On: A Loveable Lady

HEMA SUBRAMANIAM

Lovely poem!

You proved it!

Black is beautiful.

Itihas Sarwade

It's been a time loop and your are back! Very nice curation of a poem,

Really very beautiful, we were missing your peoms. Please keep posting more peoms, we would love to hear from you. Keep it up uncle

boundlessblessingsblog

Wow, brilliant poem written so beautifully for The Filmfare Black Lady Award. Too good, Shiva.

On: THE HOURGLASS

MOMENTS

A beautiful reflective poem about the passing of time and our limited existence. I like that you have chosen the image of the hourglass because it is a very visual and clear way to express your thoughts. Marta

dilkiaawazsunoblog

वक्त रेत की तरहा हतों से फिसल्ता है। हम बेठे सोचते है ये वक्त कहाँ चला है

patriciaruthsusan

It gives us an idea of how our ancestors viewed time's passing. Those are lovely hourglasses, Shiva. ☺ *— Suzanne*

www.corneliaweber-photography.com

I belong to the older generation, where as a child I was always fascinated by The Hour Glass… watching the sand slowly drop down the glass, made my time stand still… yet still to these days it hasn't changed my fascination, it is something so simple. I often get Hour Glasses as a little birthday gift to children.

Puzzles of the Soul

The hour glass certainly shows how time and our life passes so quickly.